Comptroller of the Currency
Administrator of National Banks

Real Estate Settlement Procedures

Comptroller's Handbook

September 2010

CCE

Consumer Compliance Examination

Real Estate Settlement Procedures

Table of Contents

Real Estate
Settlement Procedures

Background and Summary

The Real Estate Settlement Procedures Act of 1974 (RESPA) (12 USC 2601 et seq.) (the act) became effective on June 20, 1975. The act requires lenders, mortgage brokers, or servicers of home loans to provide borrowers with pertinent and timely disclosures regarding the nature and costs of the real estate settlement process. The act also protects borrowers against certain abusive practices, such as kickbacks, and places limitations upon the use of escrow accounts.

The Department of Housing and Urban Development (HUD) promulgated Regulation X (24 CFR 3500), which implements RESPA. The National Affordable Housing Act of 1990 amended RESPA to require detailed disclosures concerning the transfer, sale, or assignment of mortgage servicing. It also requires disclosures for mortgage escrow accounts at closing and annually thereafter, itemizing the charges to be paid by the borrower and what is paid out of the account by the servicer.

In October 1992, Congress amended RESPA to cover subordinate lien loans. HUD, however, decided not to enforce these provisions until Regulation X was amended to cover these loans. On February 10, 1994, Regulation X was amended to extend coverage to subordinate lien loans. The amendments were effective on August 9, 1994. Exemptions from coverage of RESPA and Regulation X, set forth in section 3500.5(b), were effective on March 14, 1994. Technical corrections and amendments to the rule were issued on March 30, 1994, and July 22, 1994.

On June 7, 1996, HUD amended Regulation X to clarify certain exemption provisions of RESPA, to amend the controlled business disclosure requirements, and to address specific comments raised in the 1994 rule. These amendments became effective on October 7, 1996. Congress, when it, enacted the Economic Growth and Regulatory Paperwork Reduction Act of 1996,[1] further amended RESPA to clarify certain definitions including "controlled business arrangement," which changed to "affiliated business

---

[1] Pub.L. 104-208. Div. A., Title II 2103 (c). September 30, 1996.

arrangement." The amendments also reduced the disclosures under the mortgage servicing provisions of RESPA.

In 2008, HUD issued a RESPA Reform Rule (73 Federal Register 68204, November 17, 2008) that included substantive and technical changes to the existing RESPA regulations and different implementation dates for various provisions. Substantive changes included a standard Good Faith Estimate Form and a revised HUD-1 Settlement Statement that are required as of January 1, 2010. Other technical changes, including streamlined mortgage servicing disclosure language, elimination of outdated escrow account provisions, and a provision permitting an "average charge" to be listed on the Good Faith Estimate and HUD-1 Settlement Statement, took effect on January 16, 2009. In addition, HUD clarified that all disclosures required by RESPA are permitted to be provided electronically, in accordance with the Electronic Signatures in Global and National Commerce Act (ESIGN).

Coverage (24 CFR 3500.5)

RESPA is applicable to all "federally related mortgage loans," which are defined as:

Loans (other than temporary loans), including refinancings, secured by a first or subordinate lien on residential real property upon which either:

- A one- to four-family structure is located or is to be constructed using proceeds of the loan (including individual units of condominiums and cooperatives); or

- A manufactured home is located or is to be constructed using proceeds of the loan;

and to which one of the following applies:

- Loans made by a lender,[2] creditor,[3] or dealer.[4]

---

[2] A lender includes financial institutions either regulated by, or whose deposits or accounts are insured by, any agency of the federal government.

[3] A creditor is defined in section 103(f) of the Consumer Credit Protection Act (15 USC 1602(f)). RESPA covers any creditor that makes or invests in residential real estate loans aggregating more than $1,000,000 per year.

- Loans made or insured by an agency of the federal government;

- Loans made in connection with a housing or urban development program administered by an agency of the federal government;

- Loans made and intended to be sold by the originating lender or creditor to FNMA, GNMA, or FHLMC (or its successor);[5]

- Loans that are the subject of a home equity conversion mortgage or reverse mortgage issued by a lender or creditor subject to the regulation; or

- Installment sales contracts, land contracts, or contracts for deed on otherwise qualifying residential property if the contract is funded in whole or in part by proceeds of a loan made by a lender, dealer, or creditor subject to the regulation.

Exemptions (24 CFR 3500.5(b))

The following transactions are exempt from coverage:

- A loan on property of 25 acres or more (whether or not a dwelling is located on the property).

- A loan primarily for business, commercial, or agricultural purposes (definition identical to Regulation Z, 12 CFR 226.3(a)(1)).

- A temporary loan, such as construction loan. (The exemption does not apply to a loan made to finance construction of one- to four-family residential property if the loan is used as, or may be converted to, permanent financing by the same lender, or is used to finance transfer of title to the first user of the property.) If a lender issues a commitment for permanent financing, it is covered by the regulation. Any construction loan with a term of two years or more is covered by the regulation, unless

---

[4] Dealer is defined in Regulation X to mean a seller, contractor, or supplier of goods or services. Dealer loans are covered by RESPA if the obligations are to be assigned before the first payment is due to any lender or creditor otherwise subject to the regulation.

[5] FNMA—Federal National Mortgage Association; GNMA—Government National Mortgage Association; FHLMC—Federal Home Loan Mortgage Corporation.

it is made to a bona fide builder. "Bridge" or "swing" loans are not covered by the regulation.

- A loan secured by vacant or unimproved property when no proceeds of the loan will be used to construct a one- to four-family residential structure. If the proceeds will be used to locate a manufactured home or construct a structure within two years from the date of settlement, the loan is covered.

- An assumption, unless the mortgage instruments require lender approval for the assumption and the lender approves the assumption.

- A renewal or modification when the original obligation (note) is still in effect but modified.

- A bona fide transfer of a loan obligation in the secondary market. (However, the mortgage servicing disclosure requirements of 24 CFR 3500.21 still apply.) Mortgage broker transactions that are table funded (the loan is funded by a contemporaneous advance of loan funds and an assignment of the loan to the person advancing the funds) are not secondary-market transactions and, therefore, are covered by RESPA.

Special Information Booklet (24 CFR 3500.6)

A loan originator[6] is required to provide the borrower with a copy of the Special Information booklet at the time a written application is submitted, or no later than three business days after the application is received. If the application is denied before the end of the three-business-day period, the loan originator is not required to provide the booklet. If the borrower uses a mortgage broker, the broker, rather than the lender, must provide the booklet.

The booklet does not need to be provided for refinancing transactions, closed-end subordinate lien mortgage loans and reverse mortgage transactions, or for any other federally related mortgage loan not intended for the purchase of a one- to four-family residential property.

A loan originator that complies with Regulation Z (12 CFR 226.5b) for open-end home equity plans is deemed to have complied with this section.

---

[6] The RESPA Reform Rule added the definition of "loan originator" to the list of defined terms in the RESPA regulations. A "loan originator" is defined as a lender or mortgage broker.

Good Faith Estimate (GFE) of Settlement Costs (24 CFR 3500.7)

As of January 1, 2010, a loan originator is required to provide a consumer with the standard GFE form that is designed to allow borrowers to shop for a mortgage loan by comparing settlement costs and loan terms. (See GFE form at Appendix C of 24 CFR 3500).

Overview of the Standard GFE

The first page of the GFE includes a summary of loan terms and a summary of estimated settlement charges. It also includes information about key dates such as when the interest rate for the loan quoted in the GFE expires and when the estimate for the settlement charges expires. The second page discloses settlement charges as subtotals for 11 categories of costs. The third page provides a table explaining which charges can change at settlement, a trade-off table showing the relationship between the interest rate and settlement charges, and a shopping chart to compare the costs and terms of loans offered by different originators.

GFE Application Requirements

- The loan originator must provide the standard GFE to the applicant within three business days of receipt of an application for a mortgage loan. A loan originator is not required to provide a GFE if, before the end of the three-business-day period, the application is denied or the applicant withdraws the application.

- An application can be in writing or electronically submitted, including a written record of an oral application.

- A loan originator determines what information it needs to collect from an applicant and which of the collected information it will use in order to issue a GFE. Under the regulations, an "application" includes at least the following six pieces of information: 1) the borrower's name, 2) the borrower's monthly income, 3) the borrower's Social Security number (to enable the loan originator to obtain a credit report), 4) the property address, 5) an estimate of the value of the property, and 6) the mortgage loan amount sought. In addition, a loan originator may require the submission of any other information it deems necessary. A loan originator will be presumed to have relied on such information prior to issuing a GFE and cannot base a revision of a GFE on that information unless it changes or is later found to be inaccurate.

- While the loan originator may require the borrower to submit additional information beyond the six pieces of information listed above in order to issue a GFE, it cannot require, as a condition of providing the GFE, the submission of supplemental documentation to verify the information provided by the borrower on the application. However, a loan originator is not prohibited from using its own sources to verify the information provided by the borrower prior to issuing the GFE. The loan originator can require borrowers to provide verification information after the GFE has been issued in order to complete final underwriting.

- For dealer loans, the loan originator is responsible for providing the GFE directly or ensuring that the dealer provides the GFE.

- For mortgage brokered loans, either the lender or the mortgage broker must provide a GFE within three business days after a mortgage broker receives either an application or information sufficient to complete an application. The lender is responsible for ascertaining whether the GFE has been provided. If the mortgage broker has provided the GFE to the applicant, the lender is not required to provide an additional GFE.

- A loan originator is prohibited from charging a borrower any fee in order to obtain a GFE unless the fee is limited to the cost of a credit report.

GFE Not Required for Open-End Lines of Credit (24 CFR 3500.7(h))

A loan originator that complies with Regulation Z (12 CFR 226.5b) for open-end home equity plans is deemed to have complied with 24 CFR 3500.7.

Availability of GFE Terms (24 CFR 3500.7(c))

Regulation X does not establish a minimum period of availability for which the interest rate must be honored. The loan originator must determine the expiration date for the interest rate of the loan stated on the GFE. In contrast, Regulation X requires that the estimated charges and terms for all settlement services listed on the GFE be honored by the loan originator for at least 10 business days from the date the GFE is provided. The period of availability for the estimated charges and terms for settlement services as well as the period of availability for the interest rate of the loan stated on the GFE must be listed on the GFE in the "important dates" section of the form.

After the expiration date for the interest rate of the loan stated on the GFE, the interest rate and the other rate-related charges—including the charge or credit for the interest rate chosen, the adjusted origination charges, and the per-diem interest—can change until the interest rate is locked.

Key GFE Form Contents (24 CFR 3500.7 (d))

The loan originator must ensure that the required GFE form is completed in accordance with the instructions set forth in Appendix C of 24 CFR 3500.

First Page of GFE

- The first page of the GFE discloses identifying information such as the name and address of the "loan originator," which is the lender or the mortgage broker originating the loan. The "purpose" section indicates what the GFE is about and directs the applicant to the Truth in Lending disclosures and HUD's Web site for more information. The GFE states that only the borrower can shop for the best loan and that the borrower should compare loan offers using the shopping chart on the third page of the GFE.

- The "important dates" section requires the loan originator to state the expiration date for the interest rate for the loan provided in the GFE, as well as the expiration date for the estimate of other settlement charges not dependent upon the interest rate.

- While the interest rate stated on the GFE is not required to be honored for any specific period of time, the estimate for the other settlement charges and other loan terms must be honored for at least 10 business days from when the GFE is provided.

- In addition, the form must state how many calendar days within which the borrower must go to settlement once the interest rate is locked (rate lock period). The form also requires disclosure of how many days prior to settlement the interest rate would have to be locked, if applicable.

- The "summary of your loan" section requires disclosure of the loan amount; loan term; initial interest rate; initial monthly payment for principal, interest, and any mortgage insurance; whether the interest rate can rise, and, if so, the maximum rate to which it can rise over the life of the loan and the period of time after which the interest rate can first change; whether the loan balance can rise if the payments are made on time and, if so, the maximum amount to which it can rise over the life of the loan; whether the monthly amount owed for principal, interest, and any mortgage insurance can rise even if payments are made on time and, if so, the maximum amount to which the monthly amount owed can ever rise over the life of the loan; whether the loan has a prepayment penalty and, if so, the maximum amount it could be; and whether the loan has a balloon payment and, if so, the amount of such payment and in how many years it will be due.

- The "escrow account information" section requires the loan originator to indicate whether the loan does or does not have an escrow account to pay property taxes or other property-related charges. In addition, this section also requires the disclosure of the monthly amount owed for principal, interest, and any mortgage insurance.

- The bottom of the first page includes subtotals for the adjusted origination charges and charges for all other settlement charges listed on page 2, along with the total estimated settlement charges.

Second Page of GFE

The second page of the GFE requires disclosure of all settlement charges. It provides for the estimate of total settlement costs in 11 categories discussed below. The adjusted origination charges are disclosed in "Block A" and all other settlement charges are disclosed in "Block B." The amounts in the blocks are to be added to arrive at the "total estimated settlement charges," which is required to be listed at the bottom of the page.

Disclosure of Adjusted Origination Charge (Block A)

- Block A—addresses disclosure of origination charges, which include all lender and mortgage broker charges. The "adjusted origination charge" results from the subtraction of a credit from the "origination charge" or the addition of a "charge" to the origination charge.

  - Block 1—the origination charges, which includes lender-processing and underwriting fees and any fees paid to a mortgage broker.

Origination Charge Note: This block requires the disclosure of all charges that all loan originators involved in the transaction will receive for originating the loan (excluding any charges for points). A loan originator may not separately charge any additional fees for getting the loan, such as application, processing, or underwriting fees. The amount in Block 1 is subject to zero tolerance; i.e., the amount cannot increase at settlement.

– Block 2—a "credit" or "charge" for the interest rate chosen.

Credit or Charge for the Interest Rate Chosen Note:

Transaction Involving a Mortgage Broker:[7] In Block 2, if there is a "credit or charge (points) for the specific interest rate chosen," the mortgage broker must check the box and disclose the amount of the credit or charge. The credit or charge for the specific interest rate chosen is the net payment to the mortgage broker (i.e., the sum of all payments to the mortgage broker from the lender, including payments based on the loan amount, a flat rate or any other compensation, and in a table-funded transaction, the loan amount less the price paid for the loan by the lender), excluding any fee the borrower pays directly to the mortgage broker, which is included in Block 1.

When the net payment to the mortgage broker from the lender is positive, there is a "credit" to the borrower and it is entered as a negative amount. For example, if the lender pays a yield spread premium to a mortgage broker for the loan set forth in the GFE, the payment must be disclosed as a "credit" to the borrower for the particular interest rate listed on the GFE (reflected on the GFE at Block 2, second checkbox). The term "yield spread premium" is not featured on the GFE or the HUD-1 Settlement Statement.

Points paid by the borrower for the interest rate chosen must be disclosed as a "charge" (reflected on the GFE at Block 2, third

---

[7] The RESPA Reform Rule changed the definition of "mortgage broker" to mean a person or entity (not an employee of a lender) that renders origination services and serves as an intermediary between a lender and a borrower in a transaction involving a federally related mortgage loan, including such person or entity that closes the loan in its own name and table-funds the transaction. The definition also applies to a loan correspondent approved under 24 CFR 202.8 for Federal Housing Administration (FHA programs). The definition would also include an "exclusive agent" who is not an employee of the lender.

checkbox). Block 2 cannot include both a charge (points) and a credit (yield-spread premium).

Transaction Not Involving a Mortgage Broker: For a transaction without a mortgage broker, a lender may choose not to separately disclose any credit or charge for the interest rate chosen for the loan in the GFE. If the lender does not include any credit or charge in Block 2, it must check the first checkbox in Block 2 indicating that "The credit or charge for the interest rate you have chosen is included in 'our origination charge' above," insert the interest rate and also insert "0" in Block 2. Only one of the boxes in Block 2 may be checked, as a credit and charge cannot occur together in the same transaction.

Disclosure of Charges for All Other Settlement Services (Block B)

- Block B is the sum of charges for all settlement services other than the origination charges.

  - Block 3—required services by providers selected by the lender such as appraisal and flood certification fees;

  - Block 4—title service fees and the cost of lender's title insurance;

  - Block 5—owner's title insurance;

  - Block 6—other required services for which the consumer may shop;

  - Block 7—government recording charges;

  - Block 8—transfer tax charges;

  - Block 9—initial deposit for escrow account;

  - Block 10—daily interest charges;

  - Block 11—homeowner's insurance charges.

Third Page of GFE

The third page of the GFE includes the following information:

- A tolerance chart identifying the charges that can change at settlement (see discussion on tolerances below);

- A trade-off table, which requires the loan originator to provide information on the loan described in the GFE and, at the loan originator's option, information about alternative loans (one with lower settlement charges but a higher interest rate and one with a lower interest rate but higher settlement charges);

- A shopping chart that allows the consumer to fill in loan terms and settlement charges from other lenders or brokers to use to compare loans; and

- Language indicating that some lenders may sell the loan after settlement but that any fees the lender receives in the future cannot change the borrower's loan or the settlement charges.

Tolerances on Settlement Costs (24 CFR 3500.7(e) and (i))

The RESPA Reform Rule established "tolerances" or limits on the amount actual settlement charges can vary at closing from the amounts stated on the GFE. The rule established three categories of settlement charges and each category has different tolerances. If, at settlement, the charges exceed the charges listed on the GFE by more than the permitted tolerances, the loan originator may cure the tolerance violation by reimbursing to the borrower the amount by which the tolerance was exceeded, at settlement or within 30 calendar days after settlement.

Tolerance Categories

Zero-tolerance category. This category of fees is subject to a zero-tolerance standard. The fees estimated on the GFE may not be exceeded at closing. These fees include:

- The loan originator's own origination charge, including processing and underwriting fees;

- The credit or charge for the interest rate chosen (i.e. yield-spread premium or discount points) while the interest rate is locked;

- The adjusted origination charge while the interest rate is locked; and

- State/local property transfer taxes.

10-percent-tolerance category. For this category of fees, while each individual fee may increase or decrease, the sum of the charges at settlement may not be greater than 10 percent above the sum of the amounts included on the GFE. This category includes fees for:

- Loan-originator-required-settlement services, when the loan originator selects the third-party settlement service provider;

- Loan-originator-required services, title services, required title insurance and owner's title insurance, when the borrower selects a third-party provider identified by the loan originator; and

- Government recording charges.

No-tolerance-restriction category. The final category of fees is not subject to any tolerance restriction. The amounts charged for the following settlement services included on the GFE can change at settlement:

- Loan originator required services, when the borrower selects his or her own third-party provider that was not identified by the loan originator;

- Title services, lender's title insurance and owner's title insurance, when the borrower selects his or her own provider that was not identified by the loan originator;

- Initial escrow deposit;

- Daily interest charges; and

- Homeowner's insurance.

Identification of Third-Party Settlement Service Providers

When the loan originator permits a borrower to shop for one or more required third-party settlement services and select the settlement service provider for such required services, the loan originator must list in the relevant block on page 2 of the GFE the settlement service and the estimated charge to be paid to the provider of each required service. In addition, the loan originator must provide the borrower with a written list of settlement service providers for those required services on a separate sheet of paper at the time the GFE is provided.

Binding GFE (24 CFR 3500.7(f))

The loan originator is bound, within the tolerances provided, to the settlement charges and terms listed on the GFE provided to the borrower, unless a new GFE is provided prior to settlement under specified circumstances (see discussion below, including changed circumstances and borrower-requested changes). This also means that if a lender accepts a GFE issued by a mortgage broker, the lender is subject to the loan terms and settlement charges listed in the GFE, unless a new GFE is permitted to be issued prior to settlement.

Changed Circumstances (24 CFR 3500. 2(b), 3500.7(f)(1) and (f)(2))

Changed circumstances are defined as:

1. Acts of God, war, disaster, or other emergency;

2. Information particular to the borrower or transaction that was relied on in providing the GFE that changes or is found to be inaccurate after the GFE has been provided;

3. New information particular to the borrower or transaction that was not relied on in providing the GFE; or

4. Other circumstances that are particular to the borrower or transaction, including boundary disputes, the need for flood insurance, or environmental problems.

Changed circumstances do not include the borrower's name, the borrower's monthly income, the property address, an estimate of the value of the property, the mortgage loan amount sought, and any information contained in any credit report obtained by the loan originator prior to providing the GFE, unless the information changes or is found to be inaccurate after the GFE has been provided. In addition, market price fluctuations by themselves do not constitute changed circumstances.

Changed circumstances affecting settlement costs are those circumstances that result in increased costs for settlement services such that the charges at settlement would exceed the tolerances or limits on those charges established by the regulations.

Changed circumstances affecting the loan are those circumstances that affect the borrower's eligibility for the loan. For example, if underwriting and verification indicate that the borrower is ineligible for the loan provided in the GFE, the loan originator would no longer be bound by the original GFE. In such cases, if a new GFE is to be provided, the loan originator must do so within three business days of receiving information sufficient to establish changed circumstances. The loan originator must document the reason that a new GFE was provided and must retain documentation of any reasons for providing a new GFE for no less than three years after settlement.

None of the information collected by the loan originator prior to issuing the GFE may later become the basis for a "changed circumstance" upon which it could offer a revised GFE, unless the loan originator could demonstrate that: (1) there was a change in the particular information, (2) the information was inaccurate, or (3) the loan originator did not rely on that particular information in issuing the GFE. A loan originator has the burden of demonstrating nonreliance on the collected information, but may do so through various means, including through a documented record in the underwriting file or an established policy of relying on a more limited set of information in providing GFEs.

If a loan originator issues a revised GFE based on information previously collected in issuing the original GFE and "changed circumstances," it must document the reasons for issuing the revised GFE, such as its nonreliance on such information or the inaccuracy of such information.

Borrower-Requested Changes (24 CFR 3500.7(f)(3))

If a borrower requests changes to the mortgage loan identified in the GFE that change the settlement charges or the terms of the loan, the loan originator may provide a revised GFE to the borrower. If a revised GFE is provided, the loan originator must do so within three business days of the borrower's request.

Expiration of Original GFE (24 CFR 3500.7(f)(4))

If a borrower does not express intent to continue with an application within 10 business days after the GFE is provided, or such longer time provided by the loan originator, the loan originator is no longer bound by the GFE.

Interest Rate-Dependent Charges and Terms (24 CFR 3500.7(f)(5))

If the interest rate has not been locked by the borrower, or a locked interest rate has expired, all interest-rate-dependent charges on the GFE are subject to change. The charges that may change include the charge or credit for the interest rate chosen, the adjusted origination charges, per-diem interest, and loan terms related to the interest rate. However, the loan originator's origination charge (listed in Block 1 of page 2 of the GFE) is not subject to change, even if the interest rate floats, unless there is another changed circumstance or borrower-requested change.

If the borrower later locks the interest rate, a new GFE must be provided showing the revised interest rate dependent charges and terms. All other charges and terms must remain the same as on the original GFE, unless changed circumstances or borrower-requested changes create increased costs for settlement services or affect the borrower's eligibility for the specific loan terms identified in the original GFE.

New Home Purchases (24 CFR 3500.7(f)(6))

In transactions involving new home purchases, when settlement is expected to occur more than 60 calendar days from the time a GFE is provided, the loan originator may provide the GFE to the borrower with a clear and conspicuous disclosure stating that at any time up until 60 calendar days prior to closing, the loan originator may issue a revised GFE. If the loan originator does not provide such a disclosure, it cannot issue a revised GFE except as otherwise provided in Regulation X.

Volume-Based Discounts

The RESPA Reform Rule did not formally address the legality of volume-based discounts. However, HUD indicated in the preamble to the rule that discounts negotiated between loan originators and other settlement service providers, when the discount is ultimately passed on to the borrower in full, is not, depending on the circumstances of a particular transaction, a violation of Section 8 of RESPA.[8]

Uniform Settlement Statement (HUD-1 or HUD-1A) (24 CFR 3500.8)

Section 4 of RESPA requires the person conducting the settlement (settlement agent) to provide the borrower with a HUD-1 Settlement Statement at or before settlement that clearly itemizes all charges imposed on the borrower and the seller in connection with the settlement. The RESPA Reform rule included a revised HUD-1 or HUD-1A Settlement Statement form that HUD requires as of January 1, 2010. The HUD-1 is used for transactions in which there is a borrower and seller. For transactions in which there is a borrower and no seller (refinancings and subordinate lien loans), the settlement agent may complete the HUD-1 by using the borrower's side of the settlement statement. Alternatively, the agent may use the HUD-1A. However, no settlement statement is required for home equity plans subject to the Truth in Lending Act and Regulation Z. Appendix A of Regulation X contains the instructions for completing the forms.

Key RESPA Reform Enhancements to the HUD-1 or HUD-1A Settlement Statement

While the RESPA Reform Rule did not include any substantive changes to the first page of the HUD-1 or HUD-1A form, there were changes to the second page of the form to facilitate comparison between the HUD-1 or HUD-1A and the GFE. Each designated line on the second page of the revised HUD-1 or HUD-1A includes a reference to the relevant line from the GFE.

---

[8] 73 Federal Register 68204, 68232 (November 17, 2008).

With respect to disclosure of "no cost" loans, when "no cost" refers only to the loan originator's fees (see Section L, subsection 800 of the HUD-1 form), the amounts shown for the "origination charge" and the "credit or charge for the interest rate chosen" should offset each other, so that the "adjusted origination charge" is zero.

In the case of a "no cost" loan, when "no cost" encompasses loan originator and third-party fees, all third-party fees must be itemized and listed in the borrower's column on the HUD-1 or HUD-1A. These itemized charges must be offset with a negative adjusted origination charge (Line 803) and recorded in the columns.

To further facilitate comparability between the forms, the revised HUD-1 includes a new third page (second page of the HUD-1A) that allows borrowers to compare the loan terms and settlement charges listed on the GFE with the terms and charges listed on the closing statement. The first half of the third page includes a comparison chart that sets forth the settlement charges from the GFE and the settlement charges from the HUD-1 to allow the borrower to easily determine whether the settlement charges exceed the charges stated on the GFE. If any charges at settlement exceed the charges listed on the GFE by more than the permitted tolerances, the loan originator may cure the tolerance violation by reimbursing the borrower the amount by which the tolerance was exceeded. A borrower will be deemed to have received timely reimbursement if the loan originator delivers or places the payment in the mail within 30 calendar days after settlement.

The second half of the third page sets forth the loan terms for the loan received at settlement in a format that reflects the summary of loan terms on the first page of the GFE, but with additional loan-related information that would be available at closing. The note at the bottom of the page indicates that the borrower should contact the lender if the borrower has questions about the settlement charges or loan terms listed on the form.

Section 3500.8(b) and the instructions for completing the HUD-1 or HUD-1A Settlement Statement provide that the loan originator shall transmit sufficient information to the settlement agent to allow the settlement agent to complete the HUD-1 or HUD-1A. The loan originator must provide the information in a format that permits the settlement agent to enter the information in the appropriate spaces on the HUD-1 or HUD-1A, without having to refer to the loan documents.

Inadvertent or technical errors on the settlement statement are not deemed a violation of Section 4 of RESPA if a revised HUD-1 or HUD-1A is provided to the borrower within 30 calendar days after settlement.

Average Charge Permitted (24 CFR 3500.8(b)(2))

As of January 16, 2009, an average charge may be stated on the HUD-1 or HUD-1A if such average charge is computed in accordance with section 3500.8(b)(2). All settlement service providers, including loan originators, are permitted to list the average charge for a settlement service on the HUD-1 or HUD-1A Settlement Statement (and on the GFE) rather than the exact cost for that service. The average charge also cannot be used if the charge is based on the loan amount or the value of the property.

The method of determining the average charge is left up to the settlement service provider, within certain parameters. The average charge may be used as the charge for any third-party vendor charge, not for the provider's own internal charges.

The average charge may be used for any third-party settlement service, provided that the total amounts paid by borrowers and sellers for that service for a particular class of transactions do not exceed the total amounts paid to providers of that service for that class of transactions. A class of transactions must be defined based on the period of time, type of loan, and geographic area. If an average charge is used in any class of transactions defined by the loan originator, then the loan originator must use the same average charge for every transaction within that class. The loan originator must recalculate the average charge at least every six months.

A settlement service provider that uses an average charge for a particular service must maintain all documents that it used to calculate the average charge for at least three years after any settlement in which the settlement service provider used the average charge.

Printing and Duplication of the Settlement Statement (24 CFR 3500.9)

Loan originators have numerous options for layout and format in reproducing the HUD-1 and HUD-1A that do not require prior HUD approval, such as size of pages; tint or color of pages; size and style of type or print; spacing; printing on separate pages, front and back of a single page, or on one continuous page; use of multi-copy, tear-out sets; printing on rolls for computer purposes; addition of signature lines; and translation into any language. Other changes may be made only with the approval of the Secretary of Housing and Urban Development.

One-Day Advance Inspection of the Settlement Statement (24 CFR 3500.10(a))

Upon request by the borrower, the person conducting the closing must complete the HUD-1 or HUD-1A and make it available for inspection during the business day immediately preceding the day of settlement, setting forth those items known at that time by that person.

Delivery (24 CFR 3500.10(b))

The settlement agent must complete a HUD-1 or HUD-1A and mail or deliver it to the borrower, the seller (if there is one), the lender (if the lender is not the settlement agent), and/or their agents at or before settlement. However, the borrower may waive the right of delivery by executing a written waiver at or before settlement. The settlement agent shall mail or deliver the HUD-1 or HUD-1A as soon as practicable after settlement if the borrower or borrower's agent does not attend the settlement.

Retention (24 CFR 3500.10(e))

A lender must retain each completed HUD-1 or HUD-1A and related documents for five years after settlement, unless the lender disposes of its interest in the mortgage and does not service it. If the loan is transferred, the lender shall provide a copy of the HUD-1 or HUD-1A to the owner or servicer of the mortgage as part of the transfer. The owner or servicer shall retain the HUD-1 or HUD-1A for the remainder of the five-year period.

Prohibition of Fees for Preparing Federal Disclosures (24 CFR 3500.12)

For loans subject to RESPA, no fee may be charged for preparing the Settlement Statement or the Escrow Account statement or any disclosures required by the Truth in Lending Act.

Prohibition Against Kickbacks and Unearned Fees (24 CFR 3500.14)

Any person who gives or receives a fee for or a thing of value (payments, commissions, fees, gifts, or special privileges) for the referral of settlement business is in violation of section 8 of RESPA. Payments in excess of the reasonable value of goods provided or services rendered may be considered unearned fees in violation of section 8 of RESPA. Appendix B of Regulation X provides guidance on the meaning and coverage of the prohibition against kickbacks and unearned fees.

Penalties and Liabilities

Civil and criminal liability is provided for violating the prohibition against kickbacks and unearned fees including:

- Civil liability to the parties affected equal to three times the amount of any charge paid for such settlement service.

- The possibility that the costs associated with any court proceeding together with reasonable attorney's fees could be recovered.

- A fine of not more than $10,000 or imprisonment for not more than 1 year or both.

Affiliated Business Arrangements (24 CFR 3500.15)

If a loan originator has either an affiliate relationship or a direct or beneficial ownership interest of more than 1 percent in a provider-of-settlement services and the loan originator directly or indirectly refers business to the provider or affirmatively influences the selection of that provider, it is an affiliated business arrangement. An affiliated business arrangement is not a violation of section 8 of RESPA and section 3500.14 of Regulation X if the following conditions are satisfied:

Prior to the referral, the person making each referral has provided to each person whose business is referred an Affiliated Business Arrangement Disclosure Statement (Appendix D to 24 CFR 3500). This disclosure shall specify the following:

- The nature of the relationship (explaining the ownership and financial interest) between the provider and the loan originator; and

- The estimated charge or range of charges generally made by such provider.

This disclosure must be provided on a separate piece of paper either at or before the time of the referral, or with the GFE.

The loan originator may not require the use of such a provider, with the following exceptions: the institution may require a buyer, borrower, or seller to pay for the services of an attorney, credit reporting agency, or real estate appraiser chosen by the institution to represent its interest. Further, the loan originator may only receive a return on ownership or franchise interest or payment otherwise permitted by RESPA.

The affiliated business arrangement (ABA) must be a legitimate provider of settlement services. The Department of Housing and Urban Development has issued guidelines for determining whether an ABA is a "bona fide" provider of settlement services (and thus is not a sham or shell entity organized to circumvent RESPA's restrictions on payment of fees or other compensation for the referral of real estate settlement services business). These guidelines list multiple factors that are to be taken into account in determining whether an ABA is a "bona fide" provider of settlement services. A full discussion and explanation of these guidelines is in HUD's RESPA Statement of Policy 1996-2 Regarding Sham Controlled Business Arrangements.

Title Companies (24 CFR 3500.16 and 12 USC 2608)

Sellers that hold legal title to the property being sold are prohibited from requiring borrowers, either directly or indirectly, as a condition to selling the property, to use a particular title company.

Civil liability for violating the provision that a financial institution (seller) cannot require a borrower to use a particular title company is an amount equal to three times all charges made for the title insurance.

Escrow Accounts (24 CFR 3500.17)

Effective April 24, 1995, HUD changed the accounting method for escrow accounts. HUD's rule established a national standard accounting method known as aggregate accounting. Existing escrow accounts were allowed a three-year phase-in period to convert to the aggregate accounting method. The rule also established formats and procedures for initial and annual escrow account statements (The 2008 RESPA Reform Rule eliminated provisions in section 3500.17 that related to the phase-in period for aggregate accounting, effective January 16, 2009.)

The amount of escrow funds that can be collected at settlement or upon creation of an escrow account is restricted to an amount sufficient to pay charges, such as taxes and insurance, that are attributable to the period from the date such payments were last paid until the initial payment date. Throughout the life of an escrow account, the servicer may charge the borrower a monthly sum equal to one-twelfth of the total annual escrow payments that the servicer reasonably anticipates paying from the account. In addition, the servicer may add an amount to maintain a cushion no greater than one-sixth of the estimated total annual payments from the account.

Escrow Account Analysis (24 CFR 3500.17(c)(2) and (3) and 3500.17(k)

Before establishing an escrow account, a servicer must conduct an analysis to determine the periodic payments and the amount to be deposited. The servicer shall use an escrow disbursement date that is on or before the deadline to avoid a penalty and may make annual lump-sum payments to take advantage of a discount.

Transfer of Servicing (24 CFR 3500.17(e))

If the new servicer changes either the monthly payment amount or the accounting method used by the old servicer, then it must provide the borrower with an initial escrow account statement within 60 days of the date of transfer. When the new servicer provides an initial escrow account statement, it shall use the effective date of the transfer of servicing to establish the new escrow account computation year. In addition, if the new servicer retains the monthly payments and accounting method used by the old servicer, then the new servicer may continue to use the same computation year established by the old servicer or it may choose a different one, using a short-year statement.

Shortages, Surpluses, and Deficiency Requirements (24 CFR 3500.17(f))

The servicer shall conduct an annual escrow account analysis to determine whether a surplus,[9] shortage,[10] or deficiency[11] exists as defined under section 3500.17(b).

If the escrow account analysis discloses a surplus, the servicer shall, within 30 days from the date of the analysis, refund the surplus to the borrower if the surplus is greater than or equal to $50. If the surplus is less than $50, the servicer may refund such amount to the borrower, or credit such amount against the next year's escrow payments. These provisions apply as long as the borrower's mortgage payment is current at the time of the escrow account analysis.

If the escrow account analysis discloses a shortage of less than one month's escrow payments, then the servicer has three possible courses of action:

- The servicer may allow the shortage to exist and do nothing to change it;

- The servicer may require the borrower to repay the shortage amount within 30 days; or

- The servicer may require the borrower to repay the shortage amount in equal monthly payments over at least a 12-month period.

If the shortage is more than or equal to one month's escrow payment, then the servicer has two possible courses of action:

---

[9] Surplus means an account by which the current escrow account balance exceeds the target balance for the account.

[10] Shortage means an amount by which a current escrow account balance falls short of the target balance at the time of escrow analysis.

[11] Deficiency is the amount of a negative balance in an escrow account. If a servicer advances funds for a borrower, then the servicer must perform an escrow analysis before seeking repayment of the deficiency.

- The servicer may allow the shortage to exist and do nothing to change it; or

- The servicer may require the borrower to repay the shortage in equal monthly payments over at least a 12-month period.

If the escrow account analysis discloses a deficiency, then the servicer may require the borrower to pay additional monthly deposits to the account to eliminate the deficiency.

If the escrow account analysis discloses a deficiency that is less than one month's escrow account payment, then the servicer may:

- Allow the deficiency to exist and do nothing to change it;

- Require the borrower to repay the deficiency within 30 days; or

- Require the borrower to repay the deficiency in two or more equal monthly payments.

If the deficiency is greater than or equal to one month's escrow payment, then the servicer:

- May allow the deficiency to exist and do nothing to change it; or

- Require the borrower to repay the deficiency in two or more equal monthly payments.

These provisions apply as long as the borrower's mortgage payment is current at the time of the escrow account analysis.

A servicer must notify the borrower at least once during the escrow account computation year if a shortage or deficiency exists in the account. This notice may be part of the annual escrow account settlement.

Initial Escrow Account Statement (24 CFR 3500.17(g))

After analyzing each escrow account, the servicer must submit an initial escrow account statement to the borrower at settlement or within 45 calendar days of settlement for escrow accounts that are established as a condition of the loan.

The initial escrow account statement must include the amount of the borrower's monthly mortgage payment; the portion going to escrow; an itemized estimate of taxes, insurance premiums, and other charges; the anticipated disbursement dates of those charges; the amount of the cushion; and a trial running balance.

Annual Escrow Account Statement (24 CFR 3500.17(i))

A servicer shall submit to the borrower an annual statement for each escrow account within 30 days of the completion of the computation year. The servicer must conduct an escrow account analysis before submitting an annual escrow account statement to the borrower.

The annual escrow account statements must contain the account history; projections for the next year; current monthly mortgage payment and portion going to escrow; amount of past year's monthly mortgage payment and portion that went into the escrow account; total amount paid into the escrow account during the past year; amount paid from the escrow account for taxes, insurance premiums, and other charges during the same period; balance at the end of the period; explanation of how any surplus, shortage, or deficiency is being handled; and, if applicable, the reasons why the estimated low monthly balance was not reached.

Short-Year Statements (24 CFR 3500.17(i)(4))

Short-year statements can be issued to end the escrow account computation year and establish the beginning date of the new computation year. Short-year statements may be provided upon the transfer of servicing and are required upon loan payoff. The statement is due to the borrower within 60 days from the end of the short year.

Timely Payments (24 CFR 3500.17(k))

The servicer shall pay escrow disbursements by the disbursement date. In calculating the disbursement date, the servicer must use a date on or before the deadline to avoid a penalty and may make annual lump-sum payments to take advantage of a discount.

Record Keeping (24 CFR 3500.17(l))

Each servicer shall keep records that are easily retrievable, reflecting the servicer's handling of each borrower's escrow account. The servicer shall maintain the records for each escrow account for at least five years after the servicer last serviced the account.

Penalties (24 CFR 3500.17(m))

Failure to provide an initial or annual escrow account statement to a borrower can result in the servicer (including the originator) being assessed a civil penalty of $75 for each such failure, with the total for any 12-month period not to exceed $130,000. If the violation is due to intentional disregard, the penalty is $110 for each failure without any annual cap on liability.

Mortgage Servicing Disclosures (24 CFR 3500.21)

The disclosures related to the transfer of mortgage servicing are required for first mortgage liens including all refinancing transactions. Subordinate lien loans and open-end lines of credit (home equity plans), that are covered under the Truth in Lending Act and Regulation Z are exempt from this section.

A loan originator or a mortgage broker in a table-funded transaction that receives an application for a federally related mortgage loan is required to provide the Servicing Disclosure Statement to the borrower within three business days after receipt of the application. The 2008 RESPA Reform Rule included a technical revision to the mortgage servicing disclosure statement in Appendix MS-1 of 24 CFR 3500, effective January 16, 2009. The rule streamlined the initial servicing disclosure statement language to be consistent with statutory changes.

When servicing of a federally related mortgage loan is assigned, sold, or transferred, the transferor (present servicer) must provide a disclosure at least 15 days before the effective date of the transfer. A transfer of servicing notice from the transferee (new servicer) must be provided not more than 15 days after the effective date of the transfer. Both notices may be combined into one notice if delivered to the borrower at least 15 days before the effective date of the transfer. The disclosure must include:

- The effective date of the transfer.

- The name, address for consumer inquiries, and toll-free or collect-call telephone number of the transferee servicer.

- A toll-free or collect-call telephone number for an employee of the transferor servicer that can be contacted by the borrower to answer servicing questions.

- The date on which the transferor servicer will cease accepting payments relating to the loan and the date on which the transferee servicer will begin to accept such payments. The dates must either be the same or consecutive.

- Any information concerning the effect of the transfer on the availability of optional insurance and any action the borrower must take to maintain coverage.

- A statement that the transfer does not affect the terms or conditions of the mortgage (except as related to servicing).

- A statement of the borrower's rights in connection with complaint resolution.

During the 60-day period beginning on the date of transfer, no late fee can be imposed on a borrower who has made a timely payment to the wrong servicer.

The following transfers are not considered an assignment, sale, or transfer of mortgage loan servicing for purposes of this requirement if there is no change in the payee, address to which payment must be delivered, account number, or amount of payment due:

- Transfers between affiliates;

- Transfers resulting from mergers or acquisitions of service or subservicers; and

- Transfers between master servicers, when the subservicer remains the same.

Servicers Must Respond to Borrower's Inquiries (24 CFR 3500.21(e))

A servicer must respond to a borrower's qualified written request for information relating to the servicing of the loan and take appropriate action within established time frames after receipt of the inquiry. Generally, the servicer must provide written acknowledgment within 20 business days and take certain specified actions within 60 business days of receipt of such inquiry. The written inquiry must include the name and account number of the borrower and the reasons the borrower believes the account is in error.

During the 60-business-day period following receipt of a qualified written request from a borrower relating to a payment, a servicer may not provide adverse information regarding any payment that is the subject of the qualified written request to any consumer reporting agency.

Relationship to State Law (24 CFR 3500.31(h) and 12 USC 2616)

Servicers complying with the mortgage servicing transfer disclosure requirements of RESPA are considered to have complied with any state law or regulation requiring notice to a borrower at the time of application or transfer of a mortgage.

Other state laws shall not be affected by the act, except to the extent that they are inconsistent and then only to the extent of the inconsistency. The Secretary of Housing and Urban Development is authorized, after consulting with the appropriate federal agencies, to determine whether such inconsistencies exist.

Penalties and Liabilities (24 CFR 3500.21(f))

Failure to comply with any provision of section 3500.21 will result in actual damages and, when there is a pattern or practice of noncompliance, any additional damages in an amount not to exceed $1,000. In class action cases, each borrower may receive actual damages and additional damages, as the court allows, up to $1,000 for each member of the class, except that the total amount of damages in any class action may not exceed the lesser of $500,000 or 1 percent of the net worth of the servicer. In addition, costs of the action and attorney fees may be awarded in any successful action.

Objectives

1. To determine whether the financial institution has established policies and procedures to ensure compliance with RESPA.

2. To determine that the financial institution does not engage in any practices prohibited by RESPA, such as kickbacks, payment, or receipt of referral fees or unearned fees, or excessive escrow assessments.

3. To determine whether the Special Information booklet, Good Faith Estimate, Uniform Settlement Statement (Form HUD-1 or HUD-1A), mortgage servicing transfer disclosures, and other required disclosures are in a form that complies with Regulation X, are properly completed, and provided to borrowers within prescribed time periods.

4. To determine whether the institution or its servicer is submitting the required initial and annual escrow account statements to borrowers, as applicable, and complying with established limitations on escrow account arrangements.

5. To determine whether the institution or its servicer is responding to borrowers' inquiries for information relating to the servicing of their loans in compliance with the provisions of RESPA.

Real Estate
Settlement Procedures

Appendix A

Real Estate Settlement Procedures Act Examination Worksheet

This worksheet can be used for reviewing audit work papers, evaluating bank policies, performing expanded procedures, and training, as appropriate. Complete only those sections that specifically relate to the issue being reviewed, evaluated, or tested and retain the completed sections in the work papers.

When reviewing audit or evaluating bank policies, a "no" answer indicates a possible exception or deficiency and should be explained in the work papers. When performing expanded procedures, a "no" answer indicates a violation and should be explained in the work papers. If a line item is not applicable within the area you are reviewing, indicate "NA."

Underline the applicable use:

Audit   Bank Policies   Expanded Procedures

Name of Borrower: Loan #	Yes	No	NA
1. Are written loan policies in connection with federally related mortgage loans in compliance with RESPA and Regulation X?			
2. Does the institution have established operating procedures that address the requirements of Regulation X?			
3. Are mortgage lending personnel knowledgeable of the requirements of RESPA and Regulation X?			
Special Information Booklet			
4. For transactions involving purchases of 1-4 family homes, is the Special Information booklet provided within three business days after the financial institution or broker receives or prepares a written application for a first lien closed-end loan? (24 CFR 3500.6)			
Good Faith Estimate			
5. Does the financial institution use the standard/required Good Faith Estimate (GFE)?			

6. Is a GFE of charges for settlement services, if required, provided within three business days after receipt of an application or information sufficient to complete an application by the lender or mortgage broker? (24 CFR 3500.7(a))			
7. Does the GFE appear in the exact form required by Appendix C to Regulation X? (24 CFR 3500.7(d))			
8. Does the GFE contain the following required elements:			
a. (i) Interest rate expiration date?			
(ii) Settlement charges expiration date?			
(iii) Rate lock period?			
(iv) Number of days before settlement the interest rate must be locked, if applicable?			
(v) Summary of loan information?			
(vi) Escrow account information?			
(vii) Estimates for settlement charges?			
(viii) Left-hand column on trade-off table completed for loan in the GFE?			
b. For all loans, are all third-party fees, including those paid by the financial institution in the case of no-cost loans, itemized and listed in the appropriate blocks on the second page of the GFE?			
c. Did the financial institution provide a separate sheet that identifies the settlement service providers for the services listed? (24 CFR 3500.7 and Appendix C to 24 CFR 3500)			
9. If the institution provided a revised GFE because of changed circumstances, borrower-requested changes, or interest-rate-dependent changes, did the institution issue a new GFE within three business days of receiving information sufficient to establish changed circumstances, and did the new GFE reflect only permissible changes? (24 CFR 3500.7(f))			
Affiliated Business Arrangements			
10. Does the financial institution refer borrowers to affiliated settlement service providers?			
11. If the financial institution refers borrowers to affiliated settlement service providers, is the Affiliated Business Disclosure statement provided to each borrower as set forth in Appendix D to 24 CFR 3500? (24 CFR 3500.15(b)(1))			
12. Other than an attorney, credit reporting agency, or appraiser representing the lender, does the financial institution prohibit requiring the use of an affiliate? (24 CFR 3500.15(b)(2)			

Uniform Settlement Statement (HUD-1 or HUD-1A)			
13. Does the financial institution use the appropriate Uniform Settlement Statement (HUD-1 or HUD-1A)? (24 CFR 3500.8 and Appendix A to 24 CFR 3500)			
14 Does the HUD-1 or HUD-1A contain the following? a. Charges properly itemized for both borrower and seller in accordance with the instructions for completion of the HUD-1 or HUD-1A?			
b. All charges paid to one other than the lender itemized and the recipient named?			
c. Itemized charges imposed by the lender and any sales commissions paid by the borrower or seller outside of closing, identified as "paid outside of closing" or "POC" and not included in totals?			
d. When an average charge was listed for a settlement service, was the charge calculated in accordance with the requirements set forth in 3500.8(b)(2)?			
15. From a review of the HUD-1 or HUD-1A prepared in connection with each GFE reviewed, are amounts shown on the GFE the same as the fees actually paid by the borrower? (24 CFR 3500.7(i))			
16. If a charge stated on the HUD-1 or HUD-1A exceeds the charges stated on the GFE by more than the permitted tolerance, does the financial institution cure the tolerance violation by reimbursing the borrower the amount by which the tolerance was exceeded at settlement, or by delivering or placing the payment in the mail within 30 calendar days after settlement? (24 CFR 3500.7(i))			
17. If the financial institution conducts settlement: a. Is the borrower, upon request, allowed to inspect the HUD-1 or HUD-1A at least one day prior to settlement? (24 CFR 3500.10(a))			
b. Is the HUD-A or HUD-1A provided to the borrower and seller at or before settlement? (24 CFR 3500.10(b))			
c. In cases when the right to delivery is waived or the transaction is exempt, is the statement mailed as soon as possible after settlement? (24 CFR 3500.10(b), (c), and (d))			
18. In the case of an inadvertent or technical error on the HUD-1 or HUD-1A, does the institution provide a revised HUD-1 or HUD-1A to the borrower within 30 calendar days after settlement? (24 CFR 3500.8(c))			
19. If the financial institution retains its interest in the mortgage and/or services it, is the HUD-1 or HUD-1A form retained for five years? (24 CFR 3500.10(e))			

20. If the financial institution disposes of its interest in the mortgage and does not service the loan, is the HUD-1 or HUD-1A transferred to the new asset owner with the loan file? (24 CFR 3500.10(e))			
Mortgage Servicing Statement Disclosure			
21. Does the mortgage servicing disclosure statement language substantially conform to the model disclosure in Appendix MS-1 to 24 CFR 3500?			
22. Does the lender provide the mortgage servicing disclosure statement within three business days after receipt of the application? (24 CFR 3500.21(c))			
23. Does the disclosure state whether the loan may be assigned or transferred while outstanding? (24 CFR 3500.21(b)(2))			
Notice to Borrower of Transfer of Mortgage Servicing			
24. If the institution has transferred servicing rights, was notice to the borrower given at least 15 days prior to the effective date of the transfer? (24 CFR 3500.21(d)(2))			
25. If the institution has received servicing rights, was notice given to the borrower within 15 days after the effective date of the transfer? (24 CFR 3500.21(d)(2))			
26. Does the notice by transferor and transferee include the following information as contained in Appendix MS-2 to 24 CFR 3500? a. The effective date of the transfer?			
b. The new servicer's name, address, and toll-free or collect call telephone number of the transferor servicer?			
c. A toll-free or collect call telephone number of the present servicer to answer inquiries relating to the transfer?			
d. The date on which the present servicer will cease accepting payments and the date the new servicer will begin accepting payments relating to the transferred loan?			
e. Any information concerning the effect of the transfer on the availability of terms of optional insurance and any action the borrower must take to maintain coverage?			
f. A statement that the transfer does not affect the terms or conditions of the mortgage other than terms directly related to its servicing?			
g. A statement of the borrower's rights in connection with complaint resolution?			

27. Does the institution ensure that no late fees are imposed during the 60 days following a transfer of servicing and that no timely payments are treated as late when received by transferor rather than transferee? (24 CFR 3500.21(d)(5))			
Responding to Borrower Inquiries			
28. Does the institution respond to borrower inquiries relating to servicing of RESPA-covered mortgage loans and refinancings as prescribed in the regulation? Specifically, does the institution: a. Provide a written response acknowledging receipt of a qualified written request from a borrower for information relating to the servicing of the loan within 20 business days? (24 CFR 3500 21(e)(1))			
b. If not, has the action requested by the borrower been taken within the 20 business day period?			
c. Within 60 business days after the receipt of a qualified written request, does the institution make appropriate corrections in the account of the borrower and provide a written notification of the correction (including in the notice the name and the telephone number of a representative of the institution who can provide assistance)?			
or Provide the borrower with a written explanation stating the reasons the account is correct explaining why the information requested is unavailable or cannot be obtained by the institution (in either case including the name and telephone number of a representative of the institution who can provide assistance) (24 CFR 3500.21(e)(3))?			
29. Does the institution cease providing information regarding an overdue payment to any consumer reporting agency during the 60 business day period beginning on the date the institution received any qualified written request relating to a dispute regarding the borrower's payments? (24 CFR 3500.21(e)(4)(i))			
Escrow Accounts			
30. Does the institution perform an escrow analysis at the creation of the escrow account? (24 CFR 3500.17(c)(2))			
31. Is the initial escrow statement given to the borrower at settlement or within 45 calendar days after the escrow account is established? (24 CFR 3500.17(g))			
32. Does the initial escrow statement itemize: a. Amount of monthly mortgage payment?			
b. Portion of the monthly payment being placed in escrow?			

c. Charges to be paid from the escrow account during the first 12 months?			
d. Disbursement date?			
e. Amount of cushion (24 CFR 3500.17(g)(1)(i))?			
33. Is the annual escrow statement provided within 30 days of the completion of the escrow account computation year? (24 CFR 3500.17(c)(i))			
34. Does the annual escrow statement itemize:			
a. Current mortgage payment and portion going to escrow?			
b. Amount of last year's mortgage payment and portion that went to escrow?			
c. Total amount paid into the escrow account during the past computation year?			
d. Total amount paid from the escrow account during the past year for taxes, insurance premiums, and other charges?			
e. Balance in the escrow account at the end of the period?			
f. Explanation of how any surplus is being handled?			
g. Explanation of how any shortage or deficiency is to be paid by the borrower?			
h. If applicable, the reason(s) why the estimated low monthly balance was not reached? (24 CFR 3500.17(i))			
35. Are monthly escrow payments following settlement no larger than 1/12 of the amount expected to be paid for taxes, insurance premiums, and other charges in the following 12 months, plus 1/6 of the total annual payments from the account? (24 CFR 3500.17(c)(1)(ii))			
36. Does the servicer notify the borrower at least annually if there is a shortage or deficiency in the escrow account? (24 CFR 3500.17(f)(5))			
37. Does the institution make payments from the escrow account for taxes, insurance premiums, and other charges in a timely manner as they become due or before a deadline to avoid a penalty? (24 CFR 3500.17(k))			

No Fees for RESPA Disclosures			
38. Fees in connection with RESPA disclosures			
a. Does the financial institution ensure that no fee is charged for preparing and distributing the HUD-1 forms, escrow statements, or documents required under the Truth in Lending Act? (24 CFR 3500.12)			
b. If a fee is charged for a GFE, is the fee limited to the cost of a credit report? (24 CFR 3500.7(a(4))			
Purchase of Title Insurance			
39. When the financial institution owns the property being sold, does it ensure that it does not require that title insurance be obtained from a particular company? (24 CFR 3500.16)			
Payment or Receipt of Referral or Unearned Fees			
40. Is institution management aware of the prohibitions against payments or receipt of kickbacks and unearned fees? (24 CFR 3500.14)			
41. Are federally related mortgage loan transactions referred by brokers, affiliates, or other parties? (24 CFR 3500.14)			
or Does the institution refer services to brokers, affiliates, or other parties?			
43. If fees were paid to the institution or any parties identified, were all fees paid to the broker, affiliate, service provider, or other party consistent with the requirements of 3500.14(g) and for goods or facilities actually furnished or services actually performed? (24 CFR 3500.14(g))			
44. Is the compensation received by the lender in connection with an Affiliated Business Arrangement limited to a return on an ownership interest or other amounts permissible under RESPA? (24 CFR 3500.15(b)			

Real Estate Settlement Procedures Act Forms Review Worksheet

This worksheet can be used for reviewing audit work papers, evaluating bank policies, performing expanded procedures, and training, as appropriate. Complete only those sections that specifically relate to the issue being reviewed, evaluated, or tested, and retain the completed sections in the work papers.

When reviewing audit or evaluating bank policies, a "no" answer indicates a possible exception or deficiency and should be explained in the work papers. When performing expanded procedures, a "no" answer indicates a violation and should be explained in the work papers. If a line item is not applicable within the area you are reviewing, indicate "NA."

Underline the applicable use:

Audit	Bank Policies	Expanded Procedures

Product Type	Yes	No	NA
1. Is the Special Information booklet used by the bank the most current version published by HUD in the Federal Register? (24 CFR 3500.6(b))			
2. Is the Good Faith Estimate form used by the bank the one in Appendix C of 24 CFR 3500?			
3. Is the HUD-1 or HUD-1A closing statement used by the bank the current form as contained in Appendix A of 24 CFR 3500? Any changes must conform to 24 CFR 3500.9.			
4. Is the mortgage servicing disclosure statement similar to the model disclosure in Appendix MS-1 of 24 CFR 3500?			
5. Is the notice of transfer of mortgage servicing used by the bank similar to Appendix MS-2 of 24 CFR 3500 and does the form disclose:			
a. Effective date of the transfer? (24 CFR 3500.21(d)(3)(i))			
b. New servicer's name, address for consumer inquiries, and toll-free or collect call telephone number? (24 CFR 3500.21(d)(3)(ii))			
c. A toll-free or collect call telephone number of the transferor servicer to answer inquiries relating to the transfer? (24 CFR			

3500.21(d)(3)(iii))			
d. Date on which the transferor servicer will cease accepting payments and the date the new servicer will begin accepting payments relating to the transferred loan? (24 CFR 3500.21(d)(3)(iv))			
e. Any information concerning any effect of the transfer on the availability of terms of optional insurance and any action the borrower must take to maintain coverage? (24 CFR CFR 3500.21(d)(3))(v))			
f. A statement that the transfer does not affect the terms or conditions of the mortgage, other than terms directly related to its servicing? (24 CFR 3500.21(d)(3)(vi))			
6. Does the initial escrow statement form used by the bank conform to requirements in 24 CFR 3500.17(h)?			
7. Does the annual escrow statement form used by the bank conform to requirements in 24 CFR 3500.17(i)(1))?			

Laws

12 USC 2601 et seq., Real Estate Settlement Procedures Act.

Regulations

24 CFR 3500, Real Estate Settlement Procedures Regulation (HUD Regulation X).

HUD Policy Statements

Statement of Policy 2001-1, Regarding Lender Payments to Mortgage Brokers, and Guidance Concerning Unearned Fees Under Section 8(b) (on HUD's Web site at www.hud.gov/offices/hsg/ramh/res/2001-1ltr.doc).

Statement of Policy 1999-1, Regarding Lender Payments to Mortgage Brokers (on HUD's Web site at www.hud.gov/offices/hsg/ramh/res/resp0222.cfm).

Statement of Policy 1996-2, Sham Controlled Business Arrangements (on HUD's Web site at www.hud.gov/offices/hsg/ramh/res/res0607c.cfm) (See also OCC Bulletin 2005-27).

HUD Forms

Good Faith Estimate (on HUD's Web site at www.hud.gov/offices/hsg/ramh/res/gfestimate.pdf).

HUD-1 (on HUD's Web site at www.hud.gov/offices/hsg/ramh/res/hud1.pdf).

HUD-1A (on HUD's Web site at www.hud.gov/offices/hsg/ramh/res/hud1-a.pdf).

New RESPA Rule FAQs (on HUD's Web site at www.hud.gov/offices/hsg/ramh/res/resparulefaqs422010.pdf).